Blue Flax & Yellow Mustard Flower

Blue Flax
&
Yellow Mustard Flower

poems

Alison Hawthorne Deming

Red Hen Press | *Pasadena, CA*

Book design by Mark E. Cull

Library of Congress Cataloging-in-Publication Data

Names: Deming, Alison Hawthorne, 1946– author.
Title: Blue flax & yellow mustard flower: poems / Alison Hawthorne Deming.
Other titles: Blue flax and yellow mustard flower
Description: First edition. | Pasadena, CA: Red Hen Press, 2025.
Identifiers: LCCN 2024018900 (print) | LCCN 2024018901 (ebook) | ISBN 9781636282305 (trade paperback) | ISBN 9781636282329 (hardcover) | ISBN 9781636282312 (ebook)
Subjects: LCGFT: Poetry.
Classification: LCC PS3554.E474 B58 2025 (print) | LCC PS3554.E474 (ebook) | DDC 811/.54—dc23/eng/20240429
LC record available at https://lccn.loc.gov/2024018900
LC ebook record available at https://lccn.loc.gov/2024018901

The National Endowment for the Arts, the Los Angeles County Arts Commission, the Ahmanson Foundation, the Dwight Stuart Youth Fund, the Max Factor Family Foundation, the Pasadena Tournament of Roses Foundation, the Pasadena Arts & Culture Commission and the City of Pasadena Cultural Affairs Division, the City of Los Angeles Department of Cultural Affairs, the Audrey & Sydney Irmas Charitable Foundation, the Meta & George Rosenberg Foundation, the Albert and Elaine Borchard Foundation, the Adams Family Foundation, Amazon Literary Partnership, the Sam Francis Foundation, and the Mara W. Breech Foundation partially support Red Hen Press.

First Edition
Published by Red Hen Press
www.redhen.org

ACKNOWLEDGMENTS

Gratitude to the publications where these poems first appeared.

"Galapagos" first published in New England Review

"The Gardener's Creed": *An Island in the Stream: Ecocritical and Literary Responses to Cuban Environmental Culture*, Eds. David Taylor, Scott Slovic, Armando Fernandez Soriano, New York: Lexington Books, 2019

"The Trowel" and "The Leaf": Appeared in a memorial feature in Kenyon Review online honoring W.S. Merwin shortly after his death.

"Neil Armstrong's Heart" and "Dear Moon": The anthology *Giant Steps: Fifty Poets Reflect on the Fiftieth Anniversary of the Apollo 11 Moon Landing and Beyond*, Eds. Paul Munden and Shane Strange, Canberra, Australia: Recent Work Press, 2019. With gratitude to Katharine Coles for the invitation.

"Letter to 2050": Originally published by *Scientific American*, with gratitude to Dava Sobel who curates their "Meter" feature.

"Whitewater Draw," "Wild Apples," and "National Forest": Published by *About Place Journal*. Navigations: A Place for Peace issue. Gratitude to Allison Hedge Coke.

"The Deer": Published by *About Place Journal*: The More-Than-Human-World issue. Gratitude to Nickole Brown and Erin Hallowell.

"Written on the Dark," "The Shut-Off Weir," and "Field Studies": Published in *Alaska Quarterly Review*.

"The Vocation of Care" and "Kinship with Trees and Crows": The anthology *Kinship: Belonging in a World of Relations, Vol. 5 Practice*, Eds. Gavin Van Horn, Robin Wall Kimmerer, John Hausdoerffer, Libertyville, IL: Center for Humans and Nature Press, 2021.

"Kinship with Trees and Crows": Also appeared in the online journal *Plant-Human Quarterly* out of Amsterdam.

"Views of Nature" and "The Bog": Published by the *Kenyon Review*.

"Question" and "Tannin, Sky, Night": Published in *Ploughshares*, with gratitude to Peggy Shumaker for the invitation.

"Territory Drive": Published online at terrain.org

"The Buck" and "The Bracelet": First appeared in *Cherry Tree*: A National Literary Magazine@Washington College, Issue 9, 2023

CONTENTS

I

Galapagos 15
National Forest 24
Wild Apples 26
The Gardener's Creed 27
Two Poems in Memory of Merwin
  1. *The Trowel* 34
  2. *The Leaf* 35
To My Mother's Ghost 36
Two for the Moon
  1. *Neil Armstrong's Heart* 37
  2. *Dear Moon* 39
Letter to 2050 40
At the Museum of Optics 42
Whitewater Draw 44
Desert Light 46
The Vocation of Care 47

II

Field Studies 53
Views of Nature 63
Kinship With Trees and Crows 66
Written in the Dark 72
The Shut-Off Weir 74
The Deer 75
The Bog 76
Encountering Trees 78
Question 80

III

Territory Drive 83
The Bracelet 86
Extremadura 88
The Wolves 92
Looking for Lorca 94
The Boar Hunters 98
The Buck 100
The Dulse Camp 101
The Courage of the Savannah Sparrow 114
Tannin, Sky, Night 115

IV

The Excavations 119

V

Dear America 131

Notes 139

Blue Flax & Yellow Mustard Flower

No Flowers. No us.
—Alan Dugan

All that counts is understanding whether you are managing to register, to maintain, to cherish a maximum number of alternative ways of belonging in the world.
—Bruno Latour, *Down to Earth*

I

GALAPAGOS

The relation between what we see and what we know is never settled.
—John Berger

1. *Teleférico*

First the continent rock solid at the knees
of Volcán Pichincha to begin the song
of beginnings. What soil what plants
agree to thin air two miles
above the sea which is nowhere to be seen
from this height where clouds mask range after range
that part Quito from the Pacific. Spikey grass
and tuffets of tough collective weed *azorella*
has built its own soil amassing the cushion
on which it sits waxy spears for leaves yellow asteroid
flowers a genius plant rooting on pumice decaying its way
self-composting to its future. The city diminutive below
scattered in the valley like a handful of dice and everywhere
at altitude communication towers steel gridwork
mounted with disks and drums receptors and projectors
reaching out so needful to be in touch
La Dolorosa watching from the quiet of her sanctuary.

2. *City*

What is a city?   The way we live   in our numerousness.
What is a city?   The place where water   gathers in cisterns.
What is a city?   The place where smoke   lingers on its way to sky.
What is a city?   A room in the animal house   for people.
What is a city?   The basilica where gargoyles   become real animals
    leaping from parapets   but never falling.

3. *Islands*

Whatever lives on Isabela   Fernandina   Santiago
flew or swam or drifted   on a mat of weeds   and landed
on hardened lava   ropey swirls of rock   motion frozen
but apparent   in patterns   left on black ground
where only one plant   a spindly reddish-yellow   lacework
cares to root   and rooting begins to think   this could work
the way a mind   does after thinking   I'm done there is
nothing left for me   to say or do or love   in a world of wounds
then some little tendril   reaches out   from the split seed
that a seabird has carried   by accident   in its webbed foot
and a story begins   and branches out   and finds the light
and doesn't care   how little rain   will fall as long
as it has a place   to fix itself   and sift the mist
that blows inshore   thanks to   the music of the spheres
and maybe   as the tendrils grow   they find the hostile place
has become a home   and the seed   has redefined the word it was
because all it ever wanted   was to begin again   and so

4. Iguana

Oh sure one or two beady skinned monsters
ridge backed long clawed blunt headed
might have made it floating from Ecuador on a broken tree limb
but how to explain thousands upon thousands queued up in
group salutes to the sun or lying together by dozens disguised
as rocks to spoon one spiny claw draped over the shoulder
of another and then they wake scurry in waddling gait
to water's edge dive and swim gleaning seaweed
off underwater rock adapted we say like novel to movie
from land feeders to marine machines no predatory neighbors
it's just one long beach party a sea lion or two
lumbering up to sleep on the sand good friends
says the guide about every living thing though of course
eating is a factor shark takes sea lion pup hawk takes turtle egg.
Flightless cormorants are the norm hanging out
micro-wings to dry they gave up building big wings
so easy was the catch along shore in time their prey
will learn to fear but now the immigrants make it look easy
to inhabit a place that never before was home new land
no springs no rivers just every organism's joy to thrive.

5. *Tortoise*

The mammals did not make it   maybe a mouse or rat
until people brought them   mammal to mammal transmission
whalers and buccaneers   hundreds of years of them
their graffiti still play   on the rock wall cinema at Tagus Cove
so many months at sea   they carried cows and goats and chickens
in the hold for food   barrels and barrels of water
gambling they could refill   the casks and livestock pens
as the stores fell empty but   who knew land could be so
parsimonious not a cactus   to pierce not a squirrel hare or hind
to shoot perhaps some casks   of salted fish that could be
refilled given clemency   by the sea so when they moored
in a godless place   for Europeans had forgotten
their early gods and goddesses   who live disguised
as goat or rock or laurel   and thought it took a church
to make a place holy   when they found the giant tortoises
domed carapace that   reminded them of a saddle
and made it easy   to stack the beasts
they dumped their goats   and piled up meat that could survive
a year without food or water   in reptilian cargo sleep.

6. *Judas Goat*

Abandoned goats took hold   and more they ripped
the vegetation bare   places where tree ferns
had learned to catch the fog   morning glory vines
to climb and shrubs   to fill a caldera
because land   is always learning
but had no means   without predators
to teach the goats   how to maintain
soon the horde   of ruminators turned
forest to dust   meadows to stubs
tortoises starved   died of thirst
their only water   found in plants.
All the island's labor   to make itself fruitful
required helicopter gunners   armed foot-teams and tracker dogs
a few goats got   radio collars and when they ran
to hide with kin   signaled unaware
the targets that remained   so natural history too
the epic of planetary advance   sings with calculated loss
I sing of arms and the man   but when the goats were cleared
scalesia trees   *Darwiniothamnus* shrubs
ferns and clubmoss   sang the land green again—
only the hunters   had nightmares knowing the cost.

7. *Moon*

Night on the moondeck   talk in the dark
lunar light spilling   across the calm black sea
can you professorize this grandma   why the moonlight
shines in direct line to me   *my* moon but it shines
in direct line to you too   no *my* moon so
why is that?   what is light?
wave or particle that   old beef doesn't help
it has to be about perception   something in us
that screens out   the scope and spin of space
turning the incomprehensible   turning terror into a shimmer
that spills at our feet   making the night sky
wonder what *we* are   and come close enough
          to try to see.

8. *The Guide*

His father wanted him to be a diplomat marine biologist?
what's that? three months on the beach
counting sea turtles emerging from eggs
eighty-five to a nest buried in sand
they feel vibrations from the tide then hatch
dig out and crawl to get inside the moon-riled
rhythm of the sea some went
by mistake inland to a stagnant lagoon
the student tried to save them
put them in the sea wrong the teacher said
an orientation error if repeated
in the gene chain could ruin the species.
The student ate nothing but lobsters hand-caught
for three months that's why he hates them now.

9. *Fins*

Imposters in the water we look ridiculous
but who's watching *us?* Plastic fins and masks
false skin zipped on to protect from cold
pallid faces down on the platter of the sea
we are nothing like the orange anemone
glued to rock wall combing the slosh
with its—what?— tentacles? but then again
the anemone is an animal pretending to be plant
the sea lion a mammal pretending to be a fish
the marine iguana a lizard pretending to be eel
parrot fish surgeon fish sergeant major
harlequin wrasse fakers all or so our words
would make them because we can't quite
believe the luck to be a thing with eyes
looking at anything else with eyes can't quite bear
the weight of our terrestrial burden so we float and kick
heads down imagining what we might have been or will become.

NATIONAL FOREST

Bell Rock. Courthouse Rock. Devil's Bridge.
Time has made the land forms
and they grow more beautiful with age.
Names come from the human world,
possession bleeding into perception.

What if the land had its own language?
No alphabet but steady drone
of grasslands, groan of mountains,
drought-fire's scream—a drawn-out cry,
hiss of rain, simmer of seeds

stirring restless in the soil
pure presence and process
breaking into the place
made new by cataclysm.
That's the planet speaking

and she cares about the fissures
in the dry river bed, about the lack
of ripe cherries in Washington
and blue crabs in Maryland,
savannah lions down by half.

She cares about the sunrise, dandelions,
and PCBs. She embraces whatever
we give her—blood, bone, rust
become her. She invented us
to do the work the word "care" implies,

invented us to invent words,
the thicket of endless possibilities
so death does not get the last word,
so groan and hiss could be accompanied
by our chatter, dirge, thesis, and psalm.

WILD APPLES

Henry imagined them   the apples
        that might be cultivated   from the Crab
named them in English   and Latin
        a man who possessed   a walker's appetite
filling his pockets   on the saunter out
        eating them one by one   on the return
four or five miles worth   of pocket apples.
        He believed fruits best   when eaten in the wind
one thought for the field   another for the house.
        He loved the racy   and wild American flavors
knew that Solomon says   comfort me with apples
        Homer and Herodotus   spoke of them and
the Prose Edda held   apples could restore
        youth in one   weakened by age.

Apple that grows   in the old Cellar-Hole (Malus cellaris)
        the Truant's Apple (Cessatoris)   which no boy
however late   will go by   without knocking some off
        the Chickaree-Apple   Partridge-Apple
Slug-Apple   the Concord Apple not the Discord
        the Railroad-Apple   from a core thrown out of the cars
the Saunterer's-Apple   you may lose yourself
        before you find that one   Wine of New England
the Apple where hangs   the Forgotten Scythe
        the Beauty of the Air   the Frozen-Thawed Apple
better than bottled cider   your jaws are the cider-press.
        Some brindled with red like a cow   some touched with green rust
like fine lichen.   To name them all   call in the sunrise and sunset
        call in the woodpecker   purple finch   squirrel   and jay.

THE GARDENER'S CREED

I walked with friends in Havana
and made an accidental friend—
would you like to see the garden
where Fidel preached to students—though
preach may suggest devotion to
one god over the others when
he was secular as I am—
believing in rice and corn
the stranger who became a friend
accompanying us for hours.

He took us to the garden of
laurels on campus where before
the revolution Fidel spoke
from the balcony and below
the students rallied. A bronze man
stands at the entrance—formerly
school of biology now math
which seems right when calculus of
loss seems law of nature—the bronze
Professor Felipe Aloy—

Don Felipe to fishermen
who knew him from daily visits
to the market—twenty years' worth—
when the fishes came in from boats
at noon. In 1826
he sailed to Paris carrying
85 drawings of Cuban
fishes and 35 species
stored in a barrel of brandy.
The spirit of discovery

fueled by patience and bio-love.
Friend of the fishermen he worked
in France with Cuvier and Val-
enciennes on the *Natural*
History of the Fishes (he'd
studied snails too and insects all
the unknowns of his time) all told
thus 782
new fish species from Cuban wa-
ters were added to the world's wealth.

There's more to learn than names and shapes
and habitats though knowing them
means wanting them to be: trogon,
bee-hummingbird, polymita
snail and anoles that eat them,
hutia, croc, tree-boa, kite,
the fishing bat with two-foot wings
egret, finch, flamingo, heron,
smallest scorpion in the world.
Each a calibration a cal-

culus in bone or shell or hide—
each an instrument for telling
time and knowing where they are in
space, savoring whatever form
they land in as they come to life.
Rings on clam shells and inside trees
count each year's passing with detail
on weather and hardships endured.
That's how we know, reading fossil
clams and corals that deposit

one ring of lime once each day, how
long a day is and how long
a day used to be—so puny
400 million years ago
at 22 hours. The moon
slowing Earth's rotation. I know
that numbers are numbing when what
everyone wants to feel is to
feel enough not to waste the life
of creaturely futures away.

Embargo sanction and blockade
are the language of politics
when it should be yucca, guava
sweet potato, pollo, water,
air. No one in Havana was
impressed with our dumbfounded grief,
Americans arriving with
our election still stuck in our
throats, a cry that could not quite get
past our lips so sure had we been

about loving the idea
we were the virtuosos of
democracy though the raw wounds
of civil war keep playing out
on our streets and Earth beloved
Earth denied in her need and that
was not the story we thought we
lived in, we for whom natural
beauty had been a national
creed. When we arrived in Cuba

the week of mourning had ended
Fidel everywhere—photos
lining mahogany shelves where
archeological records
and specimens were on display.
Fidel swinging a golf club then
at the Hotel Nationale
standing floor to ceiling between
antique grandfather clocks Fidel
with rifle and khaki knapsack.

People were shocked at how many
mourners amassed to pay tribute.
Sad said the drivers in vintage
cars but mounted on their dashboards
photos of their cars not Fidel.
They say we're free said our new friend
but we've had 58 years of
control and discipline. Now what
young people want is not
revolution. They want nice shoes.

After the Soviets left, Cubans
suffered. Rations meant to last
a month—rice, chicken, sugar, salt,
sweet potato (list posted on
chalkboard in tiny corner store)—
last a week and who has money?
Military and police. Don't
ask about the writers unless
you want to know silence, exile,
prison, worse. Our translator

struggled with the phrase "world of grief."
Hard to translate. *Añoranza*
he said—yearning, longing for
something past. The Edens in our
minds always egging us on to
plant and grow and weed, bending low,
kneeling down to meet the earth,
sitting to contemplate the green
that finds the spaces between stones
and leaves as they unbend, slowing

down to watch the sweet potato
vines sprawl beyond the enclosure
of the garden bed—green that finds
a ruin something to root in—
nourishment that finds a fence
something to climb for added strength,
that finds the city, whatever
ideology has raised it
or allowed it to fall, a patch-
work Eden, goodness sewn anew.

I believe in gardens. Often
I am permitted to return
to a garden as if it were
(dear Duncan's lines that are not mine
but mined to be the made place that
is mine it is so near the heart)
a stay against the sun going
down, a property of mind that
rises out of ruin so tuned
to soil is soul (call it what you

will, that stay against oblivion).
Mussels, clams, and corals grow in
tune with celestial rhythm
marking each day, a ring of lime.
What cosmic measure do my bones
take of the day and year? Surely
I am as connected to the
spheres as a mollusk. That's why I
count syllables and lines in endless
love with the metrics of connection.

We don't see beyond our pets said
Armando in *commentario,*
a lament that we build structures
animals don't understand.
The bear who eats from garbage cans,
the coyote who drinks from fountains.
We took the rivers away from them.
Our pets look at us almost asking
what we want from them. They too are
mystified by our power but

love us. I believe the garden
can sew up wounds in a city.
Words too though words can open wounds
anew. I would rather be a
woman of the corn than one of
asphalt, feel the *alisios*
blowing through seed tassels, the sea
combing words tangled in my hair
yucca bilongo paella
santería bolero eolica.

Would you like to try a 500-
year-old drink? Yes, we told our
accidental friend and walked to
the alley of outsider art
a little shrine for *santería*
sacrifice. We'd already seen
a headless rooster lying on
a curb near the police station,
Yoruba gods transported on
those hellships bound for Havana

and in the café where men smoked
montecristos we sipped shots of
bilongo—liquor fermented
from sugar and honey made by
Africans slaving to cut cane
in fields where their minds concocted
another act of transformation,
the poor man's rum—balm for the ache
of laboring, the *alisios*
brushing the skin, a lover's hand.

TWO POEMS IN MEMORY OF MERWIN

1. *The Trowel*

One day in the city there was someone on my porch
who had never been there before someone who had
written against war and for rain in the trees
someone who had asked the earth what it needed
to flourish after having been ripped raw
the market price for other ways of being.
Someone had greeted the loquat tree in my backyard
with quiet respect and admiration as I had greeted
him and the books that had become a terrarium
for me little locus of beauty to counter the decay
that seems so rank but makes soil capable of invention.
I could say he was compost to what I might hope to grow.
After dinner he saw the trowel resting on the crimson concrete
of my porch. That's a good trowel he said. The best trowel
comes from—and exacting as he was—he named the catalog.

2. *The Leaf*

The old man was telling the names
of forgotten trees
and where they had come from
an atoll a desert a temple garden.
They had all come to live with him
in a refuge for the lost
some of them the sole reminder
of their genetic kin. It was as if he knew
their family stories the immigrants
and promised to help them take root
anew. One of the trees was a Bodhi
the seed gifted to him in his travels
with a claim that it was the very tree
under which the Buddha had attained
his light. The old man raised his eyebrows
as if he knew such promises were common
among our kind though rarely could be verified.
He put the dry leaf in my hands. It was frail as lace
the color of dusk and pocked with pinholes
as it had begun to decompose. I held the leaf
and carried it from that forest from that island
across the sea to make in my home a place
for bridging the old wisdoms with the day.

TO MY MOTHER'S GHOST

The clouds surrounded me, round and white as cotton bolls. I was lost in them. It made no sense. Not a cherub in sight. The cumuli spoke in meteorological terms. They spoke my language: the material becoming immaterial.

Then you were sleeping in the pharmacological blessing of your last days, your mouth a breathing cave, your voice vanishing, throat tightening, body alien after a century of embodied dialogue. I've lost my speech, you whispered. That's alright, you don't need to talk. Two hands reaching across to take two hand in theirs.

The blanket and pillows were cotton and white as your hair, your beautiful hair which you said in your last days only I knew how to comb properly. Your hand already frail as a ghost, reaching up to smooth the part above your left eyebrow and the wave to the right, your face performing itself in an absent mirror as you did when putting on your face at your dressing table every day when I was a girl, each day a theatrical performance.

Then you were gone and I drove to high grasslands to spend the night with friends. I saw how you had whitened in the seconds after passing. And there were white crystals hurling toward my windshield. In the morning the scrub lay laced with pure white snow.

TWO FOR THE MOON

1. Neil Armstrong's Heart

At liftoff the flight surgeon
clocked his heart at a brisk walk
the explosion that forced him
away from Earth the scale
of blast that blew three
predecessors to molecular pieces
just a day at the office
to the prepared mind.

Touching down on the silver sea
Tranquility men had named it
so near to Fertility and Nectar
after alarms kept sounding
fuel enough for thirty seconds
and data overload on instruments
Armstrong's heart spiked only as his foot
hit the silky powder raced so fast

there was no time between the first
and second stroke of its beats. So
the organism registers reality even
when the mind is trained to remain
stoic as a clock. He filled his pocket with rocks
set up seismometer and solar panels
to graph granular and angular shifts
left his outer boots on the moon

in case some form of life unrecognized
and unnamed had adhered to them
and might poison life on Earth
when they returned. After scrubdown

and quarantine the moonmen were safe again
to touch and be touched. Powder so fine
the surface feels like plaster, one said.
Another: I was going to say cement.

2. Dear Moon

Spun off, kicked out, deflected space junk
little exile however you found your place
in our orbit how could we ever let you go
nameless up there in the black forever
pulling on our planet's seas and women's blood.

It was our men who made it first
envying our bodies' communion
with your magnetism. Thanks for the light
you borrowed and bounced back our way
apocalyptic fire turned by your regolith

into sheen and shapeliness, cosmetic glow—
all natural and free! No need to name a crater
Sea of Maybelline, Mare Estee Lauder.
Plato, Kepler, Copernicus, Apollo
even Jules Verne have cratered into the moon atlas.

What a conversation they must be having. Or is it
too cold up there to say a word? Maybe a little Venus
or Marie Curie would warm things up. Dear Moon,
science says you're drifting farther apart from us
but I promise you that art will never let you go.

LETTER TO 2050

The Squamscott River
   grew lazy in early summer—
muskrat rose and dove,
   heron swept the air and landed
and hemlocks that had survived
   another century's practice
of harvesting their bark
   were thriving. Some suffered
beaver girdles and the predation
   by woolly adelgids but still
the pileated woodpeckers
   found what they required
in the snags. This is how it was
   for us—pulling threads of hope
out of the air as if we had
   the skill to weave them
back into webs. We surprised
   ourselves when it worked—
so much needed to be undone.
   And I promise you that
as paltry as our efforts
   may seem to you—no.
I won't justify our failures.
   The story of the alewives'
return—that's what I wanted
   you to know because it helps
to think of desires that last
   for centuries without being
satisfied. How far inland
   did the alewives come,
I wondered, the dam removed
   after three hundred years

and in the first year then
 they came in a rush.
Locals could hear the gulls
 gathered in the estuary
in their joy and the alewives
 swam and swam to the reaches
of their ancestors—eleven miles
 and three hundred years
of appetite for place
 their genes remembered
and knew how to find.
 The Abenaki offered
a welcome back ceremony
 and fishers gathered—human,
cat and bird to feast
 and the memory that had been
thwarted for centuries
 became a fertile flow.

AT THE MUSEUM OF OPTICS

My father had an 8mm movie camera
like the one locked in a glass
exhibit box
the lens

accordioned back to collapse snug inside its case
a skin of dark brown leather
it looked like no-
thing when

closed but recorded my parents romance, the dance in
waves at Nantucket, my moth-
er flirty and
hot, surf

boiling around her white legs, long and perfect rising
to meet her floral suit, hands
at play as if
to re-

sist the splash force, eyes speaking the truth of her desire.
Eyes, yes, that brought the belov-
ed into her
neural

camera, the jazz and spark and prismatic instrumen-
tation of the brain, no brass
tubes or mahog-
any

frame, no dials or signifiers of the stars awhirl
in space. No, only a skull
full of wet con-
nections

synapses like a trillion pairs of opera glasses,
porcelain, mother-of-pearl,
rhinestone crusted,
scrimshawed.

WHITEWATER DRAW

—for Lucinda

The desolation is perfect. Vast basin.
Grasses winter dead
but golden. Morning sun
slanting to set them aglow.
Black bush. Rabbit bush.
The dead stalks of sotol.
Skeletons bleaching in desert sun.

Mountains offer lift—grey blue
haze of unattainable heights.
Sandhill cranes gather
to glean in winter. Rise and soar
and rest along water's edge
where endless drought has left
a shallow refuge they know

how to find. The voices are first
to hold the eye—songs and churrs
and calls by thousands mingled
into the pleasure to be among others
of their kind. Wings parachute
as they descend then backpedal
to ease the touchdown. Emotions

rise and call like that—a thin
voice then cacophony that makes
it hard to think. I'd bring you here
if I could, fly you across
disease ridden mountains and plains
to know this astonishment
of belonging. They lift as one,

descend, the loneliness over,
the fear of winter. During radiation
you climbed Mt. Lafayette
higher and higher over frozen
streambeds and iced rock
testing your body, knowing it,
refusing to let it be a stranger.

DESERT LIGHT

—in memory of Helen S. Schaefer

In the gold hour of desert morning
sunlight strikes the green bark
of the paloverde and what alchemy
the tree has conjured begins again
a self-renewing process that is life.

When I say strike I do not mean
a blow that wounds but like the clapper
of a bell that sends its song out
over a great distance so that it reaches
someone feeling alone and in need.

Call such translations of light and sound
a gift-giving, organic, photosynthetic,
defiant of so much that is cruel.
This Helen launched no ships
bound for war but her presence

could disarm a bully and embolden a poet.
She understood that art is necessary
and rare. She gave it room to grow.
What consolation can there be for death
but leaving behind so much to treasure.

THE VOCATION OF CARE

—Archibald MacLeish Field Station
Northampton, Massachusetts

Someone has tied dozens of stones
to the limbs
of the London plane tree

white string glued to rocks
clipped with clothes pins
forcing the limbs to fountain

down toward the bed of mulch.
I can't tell if the work is
science or art though it makes me

think of Rene Dubos and
The Wooing of Earth
how we love tended nature

more than the wild. Spindly chestnut trees
sprout in the seed orchard
an experiment blending bacteria

into the genome to quell
the toxin that killed
the forest ancestors.

My grandfather, taciturn Yankee doctor,
preferred plants to people.
Luther Burbank type.

Carried a little pot of hot wax
tied to his belt
for grafting fruit trees

hoping pears and apples
might be coaxed
from the same wood.

His office sat next door
to a water-powered mill.
Connecticut industry

ran on water. Clockmakers
hatmakers, axe and gun makers.
He must have treated

arms yanked out of joint
on a fly wheel, fingers
lost to blade or gear. Worse.

I picture him walking
the woods of my childhood
with my father, the two men

gentling the leaves of trees
they knew would die.
He'd have been happy

to see the new science
mend some wounds
he'd been unable heal.

He'd love this closet
full of off-duty
microscopes lined up

on the shelf each wearing
                    a cowl labeled Leica
          cloistered like monks in lambent prayer.

II

FIELD STUDIES

—Bowdoin College Scientific Station
Kent Island, New Brunswick, Canada

1. First, There Was an Albatross

Ernest Joy spotted the bird
lost or adventuring from
south of the equator, spied it
flying offshore from Wood Island
the yellow-nosed albatross
rare in the North and close enough
to shoot as naturalists in his day
did so numerous were the furred
and feathered and finned. Joy gave
the bird to Allan Moses, island naturalist,
skilled at taxidermy who knew
the Museum of Natural History
would want the skin for study
and so traded it for passage
to a Congo expedition hunting
Grauer's green broadbill
to fill the museum's collection.
The team crossed Lake Tanganika,
traversed the plateaus of Marungu,
sailed north to Uvira, trekking
by foot with a caravan of porters
into the upper Congo forest.
Moses found the bird feeding
on berries in a vine-draped tree
while others were off in the bush.
They returned to find Moses
asleep in his tent, green broadbill
lying dead on his chest. With what
satisfaction, they wrote, we proceeded
to dissection! Moses complained.
All this for one dead bird? (935 birds

to be exact.) Will you do nothing,
he complained to his sponsor,
for the eiders back home on Kent Island?
Mere finger of grassy meadow and
rocky shore safe enough for nesting.
First, came the albatross,
though it knew nothing
of the human story that remains.

2. Navigation of the Leach's Storm Petrel

Science wanted to know
what they know, sooty little
tube-nosed ocean runner,
fork-tailed forest-burrower,
night wanderer, transient in
the sweet musk of woods.
How do their find their way?
What's their sense of place?
Do they know a sense of
belonging when they return
from a year at sea to breed
in the forest where they hatched?
Or is it just work to repair the burrow?
They stagger around at night
on forest paths. They don't
understand the land
but they need it. A man
who studied the colony
for half a century took
some petrels to Ireland
to see if they could find
the way back. First bird returned
before the man did. Was it
nine days or thirteen?
Do the numbers matter
when the bird just knew,
its inner compass reading
longitude and latitude, skirting
open ocean swells to arrive
where it knew it should be?

3. *Site Fidelity of the Leach's Storm Petrel*

At night the pairs chuckle and purr
sometimes in harmony
nestled in their burrows
ghosting the forest with
their chatter. They have a lot
to say after spending so long
in solitary flight with nothing
on their minds but light
and wind and the scent of prey
that draws them onward.
They might fly four hundred
kilometers from land
seeking lanternfish and krill,
loading oil to bring home
for the chick. They winter
at sea flying as far as South Africa,
intimate only with water
until some brain or body switch flips.
Who can explain the call
for another, the call for home?
Together again, same time,
same place, next year,
more faithful to burrow
than to spouse, grooming
the nest with soft leaves,
fresh grass, they talk
and talk throughout the night.

4. Petrel Chick

What did I know
lying in the darkness
where I had hatched?
At first I loved the smell
of loam, musk, the dampness
of the underneath. Then came
a fishy scent though
what did I know of fish?
Bill to bill my lunch
was served. I had no
control over where
I lived, when or what
I ate. But sufficient
to my status as a puff
of proto-feathers the meals
kept tunneling down
from the spot of light
at burrow's end. I knew
to raise my mouth
to what arrived.
I had no idea what I was
or what I was meant to be.
Ridiculous, I know, that
I should have a voice.
Sleep and eat and roll over
in the earthen dark
that was life until
I grew so blubbered
I could barely turn in my sleep.
I squeezed out of that earthhold

when I caught the open ocean scent
that told me I had wings
and I was gone into
sea-spangled spume and sky.

5. *Parent-Offspring Conflict*

We take turns leaving the nest
to forage, one fasting
the other flying as far
as it takes, Georges Bank
or Cape Cod, to gorge
on krill for the little one
and the mate we've left behind.
Sometimes out there
in the beyond with no
markers of time and place
it just feels right to keep going,
the forest burrow, a bother
all duty and constraint.
Besides we live so long
we barely age at all.
Telomeres, biologists say,
fragment as they age.
Not ours. So what
does it matter if this year
one bird does not go back?
There will be more chicks
and more. Some years
we get out there in the grey
where the sea and the sky mix
and the land—what is land?
This year it's all about flight.

6. Floral Constancy of the Bumblebee

Flowers because they are grounded
in earth have an electric field
around them, the biologist says,
fact becoming poem. She studies
how bumblebees learn
what flowers to visit for nectar.
Transects map the pollinator
network of the island. Leafcutters,
she says, make sleeping bags
from circles they cut from rose leaves.
Sweat bees, she says, favor
Queen Anne's lace. If you are a bee,
she says, visiting hawkweed,
yellow rattle, dewberry, milkweed,
blueberry, clover, and vetch
you need to learn with each flower
how to get down into the sweet.
But if you specialize on one
blossom shape you can get
right down to business.
A good plan, she says,
because it takes a while to learn
how to handle a flower.

7. Learning in the Savannah Sparrow

Bird brain, we humans say,
to put someone down. But try
making a nest in the grass
on an isolated northern archipelago,
raising your chicks in the open
where gulls and ravens prey.
Try flying on the power of your
thin feathered arms to spend winter
in a southern clime a thousand miles away
then flying back to the same meadow
to mate, knowing how to avoid
close relatives for pairing,
the whole cycle playing like
an earworm year after year,
and each summer learning
the song the meadow is singing
and carrying that tune
with you wherever you go.

8. Fog Heaven

Being a matter
of numbers and vials
the cloud physicist
found it
easy to live
in a cabin the size of
a heavy stillness
that wants
to dissipate.
He mastered the art
of bottling fog.
I slept with his ashes
perched on a shelf
no one ready
to let him go.
But the stars
kept waking me
or was it
the ghost asleep
in the corner
wrapped in tin foil
as if to protect him
from too much light
and lush night
upon me like
moss on a forest log.

VIEWS OF NATURE

—after Alexander von Humboldt

Von Humboldt wrote
that the ancient mind
didn't much care

for nature—the thing itself—
instead filling sea and land
with symbols of human power and fear

projecting gods and goddesses
onto the stars with names
that remain our own.

The Greeks lived he said
on wood-crowned cliffs
along deeply indented shores

ineradicable ever-springing waters
olive trees hovering like light fog
over the mountainsides

yet the ancients he said did not *feel*
the place—workshop of clouds
the eggs of plants

that are sent with crowns of hair or feather
upon long autumnal journeys
creatures living within

the fluid of fisheyes
the gills of bream
the limestone temples

built from skeletal fragments
        (biogenic precipitation
                falling in seawater) mollusks

corals and foraminifera.
        And when Homer paints
                the island home of Cyclops

his purpose is nothing more
        than to bring before our eyes
                the abundance of the wild dwelling place

of monsters. When Sophocles
        places Oedipus in verdant darkness
                thick embowering ivy and golden-

bearing crocus it's not to glorify
        the repose of nature but to heighten
                the pain of blindness and exile.

Von Humboldt was first to write
        of the world as Earth's
                possession not ours

life as a breath that
        came from Earth itself.
                He never mentioned God.

He saw life pouring
        over rock from pole to pole
                igniting in us

an imaginative force
matching nature's fervor
the whole bound together

in a netlike intricate fabric
nature no backdrop
to the story but its maker.

KINSHIP WITH TREES AND CROWS

To be rooted is perhaps the most important and
least recognized need of the human soul.
—C.D. Wright

When I think about what I miss most

what I wish to be in conversation with

at my summer home in eastern Canada

from which I'm exiled by the pandemic

and our government's failure

to protect our people unlike our kinder

northern neighbors who have done well

to shelter themselves and each other

what I miss most, calling to mind the land

I've known since I was a child,

are three smart trees and a kindness of crows.

I refuse to call them a murder. I wonder

if they sense my absence? The crows

I mean. Should be the same population

summer after summer that speaks

in my dooryard, the caw-caw of their

intelligence familiar and inscrutable to me
yet familial. When I arrive I see five or six
gathered in the tamarack snag that I call
the Crow Tree. They love its bare
upper branches reaching as if choreographed
to gesture for the sky, one arm straight,
the other bowed so that together
they look like some kind of implement
a primitive pitchfork or a partial trident
or a giant's gaff hook. You get the picture.
I'll throw a caw or two or five
in their direction, trying to match the number
of times they iterate the syllable. That's about all
we can say to each other. They pretend to ignore me.
But I know they know me and that I am part of
the rhythm of their year as I arrive and plant seeds
and spread some extra for them to eat. That snag

is the first of my three smart trees. It refuses
to fall, dead now for a decade and its companions
long cleaned out with chain saw and splitter
after the infestation of bark beetles turned
a forest into a field of death. Our pandemic
is novel only to the human eye. Even the crows
suffered such a scourge when the avian flu
burned through them like wildfire. That's when
ornithologists learned that no crow dies alone
a companion always by the side of one dying.
The tamarack has a purpose as launch pad
for crows, as object of my admiration,
as place of reverie and prospect
for all of us in the small interspecies
family who dwell here. Then there's
the black spruce, a lone survivor
of predation's purge, a tree too broad

for my arms to encompass. During
the purge it lost its spire, standing
blunted and doomed for years
telegraphing crown decline which I
took to be a sign of its death.
But slow by slow the spruce trained
an upper limb to migrate from
horizontal to vertical. It seemed
as surprised as I was at this sign
of vitality. The makeshift spire
sprouted a mass of fresh cones
a gonadal extravagance or boast
that filled me with a strange erotic
joy. Finally, the old cedar, rare on this
working island where fence posts
and shingles have been the plight
of cedars for two hundred years.

I imagine the farmer who once owned
this land prized the copse of cedars
rising up from swampy ground
at the perimeter of his stable corral.
Oh but that's history when I've been
on this land for more than sixty years
the farmer and stable gone decades
before that. But the cedar's hung out
for all the transitions, from my childhood
laughter to my old age astonishment
to still be alive and well and rooted here
even if seasonally transient. I like the way
the cedar is dying. It's been leaning
seaward year by year, now at forty-five
degrees from fallen. Its root-ball
is lifting and along its skyward
flank new branches have sprouted.

It's reaching for light but I think also
working to counter gravity's pull
preparing to become a nurse tree
when it finally loses its grip. The death
will be gentle though the force
of such a weight hitting the ground
will echo and make stones tremble.
There will be a whoosh when the still
green branches touch down as they ease
the last passage from a life seeking light
to one embracing dark loam of earth.

WRITTEN IN THE DARK

I sit in the fog on a small island in the North Atlantic
a peaceful day with the invasive leopard slugs
destroying my lettuce plants
invasive green crabs decimating the clams
that thought they'd lie at peace in mud.

Tent caterpillars are having a good summer
devouring trees on the mainland
though a surprise fungus may be
slowing their spread while on the island
the forests work to recover

from last year's bark beetle assault
that tore through like a wildfire
turning giant black spruces and lacy tamaracks
into spindle-stick corpses. The ash trees
so far holding out against emerald ash borer.

So now I read about trees and praise the knowledge
their bodies archive. Nickel-harvesting species
that grow in mine tailings—"hyper-accumulators"
that suck up waste that becomes
batteries to drive our cars,

soil made clean for crops, trees become central characters
in the human drama, carbon consumers and altruists
nourishing one another through roots,
code talkers who send chemical messages
when parasites rise.

One day when working in the woods
I heard a stand of white birches call out to me
across a fern meadow. I understood them
to mean that they wanted to be seen
as light having an edge over darkness.

THE SHUT-OFF WEIR

Getting ready for bed   I noticed lights on the water
a boat working   along the island shore.
Was it search and rescue?   Boats leaving
the North Head wharf   head east or northeast
to herring weirs   or salmon cages.
This boat had come south   to the Long Bank
and it made no sense   in a place where
tides and fish determine   where the boats will go
patterns of routine behavior   reminding me of the fish biologist
who described the largest   migration in the world
happening every night   when plankton rise from the bottom
and come to shore to feed.   Herring follow them.
And so the boats and so   the islanders lining the scenic
pullout to behold the work   trucks, camp chairs, and binos.

Next I could see someone   had cast twine in a broad arc
across the little cove.   By six a.m. the gulls were screaming.
By afternoon two carriers   lay back waiting to fill
their holds. A couple skiffs.   Someone at the pullout said
I heard they could get   a thousand hogsheads. Another said
three thousand. A fish story   forming as the boats
drew the sweep across the weir   to push the herring
into the pocket.   Wind picked up.   Someone said
easterly wind is a cancer to that weir.   No one had fished
this method for decades.   Maybe someone's father knew
how to do it but others   from a nearby island had come
to help and so it went.   The crowd grew and with it
the stories flowed.   What seemed lost knowledge
came back   and as in those days   abundance ruled.

THE DEER

She browsed beneath the wild apple tree
that stands outside the windowed wall
beside my dining table. She lifted her head.
Eyes onyx. Eyes glass. Eyes blank screen.
What processor, what operating system,
what leap-the-gap impulse turned
her looking my way and made her stay?
I stayed too, eye to eye, we held the space
between us like a coin we'd never spend.

THE BOG

The pond flooded over its banks
when winter storms heaped gravel
blocking its outlet to the sea.
Peat-rich water rose to drown
sheep laurel, Labrador tea,
pitcher plants, dragon mouth
orchids and wild cotton
all rarities of the bog lands.

Another summer and the ache
of grey twigs encircled
the pond and some tall spruces
ghosted the landscape where once
they crowned it. I came to see
how much would sprout back
now that another winter
had burst open the outlet

the flood subsiding. These plants
know the cyclical violence
of flood, drought, ice. The tall
salt grasses greened up first
dressing the mud hummocks
like party clothes. The Labrador tea
began to pop green buds
from its extremities. The spruces

in time will fall but their cones
lie prepared to be broken into growth.
Repair takes time, it has a rhythm
like the sea, swelling up, pulling back.
Everything that lives understands

this rhythm, but who doesn't need
to see the signs to remember
it is the way of the world to mend.

ENCOUNTERING TREES:
Red Trail from South West Head to the Whistle

Old birches lead complicated lives.
One falls in a gale then lying on its side
feels sun on its bark and begins
a new branch that becomes a trunk
and rises. Another grows a knee
for support after wind has made
it kneel. One grows an elbow for reclining
as it leans from vertical to horizontal.
Another grows a looping branch
like the curve in a jump rope
turning an obstacle into a game.
But the grandmother tree is the marvel
sprawling like an obese queen
trunk split like a woman's cleft
side branches snaking low
to reach beyond the canopy
skototropic as a tropical vine
that reaches into darkness
to find its way to light.
A tree that is a community of trees
a tree that refuses damage
turning storm and infestation
into a form that grows stronger
for all it has suffered. Grandmother,
I have walked through a dark forest,
red needled and lit with ghost flowers—
Indian pipes we used to call them
as if to see them were to hear
the land's indigenous music.
At dawn I sat on a rotting log
and read *The New York Times*
on my smart phone, America

still going to the mean dogs.
Squirrels scolded, chickadees fed,
a noisy mob gathered in the spruce,
and the bald eagle remained
out of sight. What is it to endure
but to feel the cadence of uncertainty
accepted as the condition for growth?

QUESTION

What bird
was that
that just
flew through
my mind?

III

TERRITORY DRIVE

I went for a walk again today over the hilly street
    bordering my subdivision
                    went a mile
        to where the street splits
                then climbed to where
    the median strip
                shelters brittlebush
            and penstemon
                    in wild bloom and
there where the road split
                I was relieved
        of commodity and commerce
                    as the street was relieved
    of our customary speed
                to get somewhere.

The air was mild   the sun sharp
            desert light   intense
                as is   my isolation
    made requisite   by a being   or is it
            a non-being   dispersing
        in the global   humanosphere
noncellular   nonmetabolic   unable to grow
            or replicate   without a host
    crumbled bunch of twine   oily membrane
        protein spikes that   Velcro to human lungs
                the virus needs us   and we
        the numerous   comply

or not
walking alone noting
pleasures in the familiar that we had
once found abroad
Lyon's silk looms
the Alhambra's heavenly garden of Islam
Delphi's mystic air
now it's mica flecks
in roadside gravel
little stars in the firmament
of what keeps us grounded
when the angst makes us spin.

I don't know how
to speak of grief I feel
the floor
break open beneath my feet fall into
abysms of the unthinkable just imagining
my daughter my grandsons . . .
but seeing the semis
lined with quick-built
wooden shelving
stacked with white-wrapped
corpses
the sheen and contour of the shrouds
I force myself to write
learning to see
each one of them as among my beloveds
each word an act
of defiance against the unspeakable.

I walked out and returned
the phainopela
churring from atop the leafless mesquite
fearless in its black satin camo
matchtip flames atop ocotillos
the yardman
loading his trailer
with pulled weeds ring of shovel
scraping dirt

then heart swelling
at scent of orange blossoms
neurologic memo to the sense of smell
a paean to hope that my body
my brain can still equate with
spring and all
while the neighborhood
contracts behind disinfected doors
and we winter ourselves
keeping the difficult distance.

THE BRACELET

His parents had spent six years in Bergen-Belsen
father a baker each night stuffing a loaf

in each pant leg bringing it to the barracks.
He played violin for Nazi dancers.

Mother sewed their uniforms. One day an officer
threw her into a machine that took off her

wedding band finger. The man who sat beside me
had seen a photo of his mother holding him

when he was a baby that finger missing.
Women, other prisoners, mended the wound

stitching the gap where the finger had been.
Stranger to stranger the story unwound

like a spool of thread. The repair was ragged
but she left the scar that way. Before she'd been taken

to the camp she'd given a gentile friend
three treasures a gold bracelet

links too heavy to wear (it must have weighed
three or four pounds he said a way to save the wealth)

plus a ring and a rose gold watch that hung on a necklace.
This was 1939. Six years later they were liberated.

One man weighed sixty pounds. When the baker ran up
to embrace the British liberator the soldier said

he could barely feel   the man in his arms
so near had he come   to being a skeleton.

His parents returned   to their village
found the gentile woman.   She gave back

the bracelet and the ring.   The necklace
with pendant watch   she'd had to sell for food.

No recrimination   in my seatmate's voice
who told me he kept   the bracelet in a safe deposit box

as I have kept his story   in these broken lines
to make of them   something almost whole.

EXTREMADURA

Madrid.   I stand in the sun
        surrounded by   armed guards
                waiting for clearance
                                        layer upon layer

all secured behind
        the American Embassy's   glass and protocol
                then
            conversation and lunch

no ambassador.   The American president
                doesn't want one.
                                Diplomatic smiles.

I've come to Spain
                to talk to scholars
                                about animals
        to talk to students
                        about poetry and science

to listen   to history   if it will speak.
        My host says Spaniards   are not
                xenophobes   even after
        the Atocha   attack.

What troubles them   is when
        a father   takes his daughter
                out of high school   saying
        she's had enough education.

❀

Fuenlabrada.   The School of
Joaquín Araújo
poet and naturalist

who wrote of the possibility
of being instructed
in the essential
by the essential.

Naming is   the start
of school   the person or place
that grounds a child.

Towpath   the school
where   I began
where mules
towed barges
along a canal
town to town
granary to tobacco shed
mill to axe factory

vernacular landscape
before the beige   strip malls
bled the colors   out of the land.

The essential is the whole
is the liveliness
all that trees   have given us.

These kids   are from everywhere
the displaced   trying to figure out
where they belong.

I show them an Oregon forest
Death Valley
marine iguanas of the Galapagos

and I read them poems
emerged from those places.
They cheer
like I'm a rock star.

I never thought of that a boy tells me
making poetry out of science.
Try it I tell him
hoping language
is a new place he can belong.

❀

Atocha Station. Glass monument
to bomb victims
two hundred killed

then the worst terrorist attack
in Europe the terminal
now all foodissimo and churros
ear buds and shades

no scanners or guards
just a queue
for the slow train
to Extremadura.

❀

Passing through fields
painfully green
the breakage of early spring
shoots piercing ground

grasslands mile after mile
a tended landscape
cloudbursts of mustard flowers

dirt etched by cultivator blade
black pigs free-range
rooting under oaks for *bellotas*

red fox nose to wind
taking the moment
for all

olive trees their haze of silver-
green thought
riding the swales as if the groomed land

were a sea
and the trees were
passengers
riding the easy swells
enjoying the view.

THE WOLVES

A man told me this story   at the conference dinner
          big round table   with talk of books
     much wine   *queso y jamon* to start.

We shared an elegant salad   meant to be shared
     vegetables built   into a turret
we dismantled   and placed   on our plates

bits of partridge nestled   in the leaves.
          Are they wild? I asked.   Not this time of year.
     Wild ones leave buckshot   in your mouth.

     Narrow pointed red peppers   *pimientos?*
          stuffed with cod.
The man had grown up   during Franco's regime

his father returning   from service
     in the civil war.   There were no jobs.
He found work   cutting wood

     Franco's plan to build   water works that even
          after all   the cruelty
     people see   was a good deed.

The man   a Spanish scholar   of American lit
     then a boy   remembered how
          the family had moved   hut to hut

in the woods   building a new shelter
          as the cutting   progressed.
     They lived on rabbits   lizards and frogs.

The meal and the wine   went on and on
fish wrapped in   thin strips of zucchini
fig ice cream with currants

chocolate grenache   *bellota* liqueur
and joy in conversation.   We had gathered
to talk about animals   and what kind of animal

we humans might be.   Mother tamped down
the cook fire.   Father slept off the ache
of labor.   Love kept us alive, he said.

He had heard   as a boy   half asleep
on forest ground
the wolves howl   (sing I think he said)

and he was not afraid.   Hearing him
seeing the love   (the man's name was Jesús)
on his face   I thought again

maybe the animals   who were the first gods
in the childhood   of humanity
might be the last gods   in our desanctified world.

LOOKING FOR LORCA

the *vega* lined with orchards
trees set like beach umbrellas
as shelter from high sun

trading sugar beets
the land between snow and wheat
for the *vega* inside him *the lily*

impossible to water
man made to desire
and never have his desire fulfilled

blessed by the shadows of mules
sacks full of sunflower seeds
the river he sat beside as a child

the birds he listened to
teaching him poetry
a cascade that flows

from mountain to stream
too many rills to name
though someone thirsty

can dip a clamshell to drink.
Maybe that's the poet's way of knowing.
The farmhouse where he was born

clay *ollas* to gather water
grain stored upstairs
house as barn with weighted drapes

photo of Lorca at keyboard
vase of flowers resting above
left hand on the score

right on the keys same piano
same vase here now as in the photo
mother reading Victor Hugo aloud

boy playing hide and seek
here comes the wolf
he quivered in fear

shepherds fields sky
he followed the plow
the blade's cut bloodless

turning up roots.
Once the plow unearthed
a Roman mosaic

his first artistic marvel
the second gitano songs
he knew the outcast's pain

his third Madrid
where he found people
who walk just to walk

fill the bars just to fill the bars
where he found the stage
the truck the transport

bringing classics to villages.
¿Qué es la vida? Un frenesí.
¿Qué es la vida? Una ilusión,

una sombra, una ficción,
y el mayor bien es pequeño:
que toda la vida es sueño

a man who fell in love as easily
as the breeze falls for the trees.
Water had come deep inside him

the riffs and *martyrdom of water*
. . . water that
suffers and weeps

full of tiny white violins.
Ah profane soul of water
that lives by fugitive law.

Sebastian was his saint
his serenity in the midst
of misfortune.

He saw the Civil Guard
kill a gypsy
each day and write down

the name on a long
undulating list like
a Chinese dragon.

They came to his door
led him to the olive grove
I pray Saint Sebastian was with him

moonlight slipping through
the latticework of trees.
In one of the last photos

he wears a white linen suit
sitting at a sun splashed plaza café
carafe of water empty glass

see how black his eyes are
lit with brilliant night
he has just noticed the wine glasses

hanging above the bar
as if *canaries flying*
amid the tapers.

THE BOAR HUNTERS

The Americans have come down from the mountain
to have beer and food with their Spanish guide
in a brick tavern perched over the River Darro.
The man is high from killing, too loud
for an intimate space that feels more like a cave
than a restaurant. And all caves have duende.

But the American killer has none. He has
a loud voice and a compliant wife
and a guide he does not realize
is mocking him. Or maybe their exchange
is some kind of masculine preening.
I don't know but I worry for the woman

as she plays almost well the role her husband
has cast for her. He hates the goat cheese
in the *milhejas de mango y queso de cabra*
y miel de flores his guide has ordered for him
a local delicacy. He hates the lamb.
The Spaniard says the dish is a small bomb.

He watches it go off at the table. The couple
talk about all the animals they want to shoot.
Moose and bison and boar. The man is all boast—
keeps giving the moose call. He wants to be heard.
He wants to be smarter than his host. Richer.

I've made a lot of money looking people in the eye.
He gives even me the old broad with the notebook
the look. Epic fail, dude. The wife's nervous giggle
never stops. She says I want to kill a bison
I want to climb a mountain and kill an ibex.
She will die a little with everything she kills.

He keeps digging himself a deeper hole.
Wisconsin cheese, now *that's* good cheese.
The Spaniard doesn't flinch. Maybe I can take you
to the caves where they make blue cheese. Fungus
and flies land on it. On your plate it looks like brown liquid
falling slowly down. If you eat it, it's delicious.

THE BUCK

The Bighorn Fire came within a mile of my house.
It owned me for several weeks. The smoke
stopped my daily walks and kept windows
closed day and night. Go-bag ready, I watched
the mountains, fireline brilliant orange
against char of night, as the blaze
snaked along the ridge in its advance,
closer and closer, then farther and farther
as crews turned the fire, driving it away
from our homes. The buck made his way
from Doug firs to townhomes,
over four-foot brick wall to my birdbath.
I caught him on a field cam after my swiss chard
and lettuce were chomped to the nubs
and I couldn't picture what creature
could wreak such damage. But when
I imagined the cost for him to grow
the six-point rack that shone in the photo
like branches of a moonlit tree, when
I imagined the thorny scrub he'd fed on
as he fled his range, and then his pleasure
finding tender green leaves, new to his palate,
soft on his lips, yielding to blunt teeth,
I felt the fool—no—criminal for thinking
him the thief when our kind has stolen
nearly everything from the animal world.

THE DULSE CAMP

—after lines by Seamus Heaney & Elizabeth Bishop

1.

I'd come to the seawall
soothed by just looking,
climbing on tumbled rocks
the sea had laid to form
a curving spit.

I found the shacks
of dulse pickers leaning
into blocking that once
had held them square.
Rusty winch and cable

lying idle. A stream
cuts through woods
to feed the pond
the seawall's made
and beyond

open water always
right for longing
the shimmer and reach—
channel cleaving
two nations. No border

can be drawn on water
as if to say no contest
just a rip and tidal pull
deeper than all the history
that produces flags.

I found a battered aluminum
channel marker fixed
to its pole washed up
on shore. I took it
to mark the doorstep

at the dulse camp
that stands on land
not owned, deeded, taxed
but cobble made
and kept by the sea

a place existing free
of logic and law.
Whatever use the camp
might have, say,
resting after hard labor,

brewing up black tea,
waiting for dulse to dry,
maybe just sitting
to watch the heron
watch the water's surface,

teeters on the brink.
Wrack of timber, plank,
and broken-handled gaff,
plastic water bottles
shiny as rain, polystyrene float

like a chunk of yellow blubber,
trap lines and mooring lines
washed up like gale-wracked weeds,

toy tractor some kid
dropped overboard wondering

would it float. Endless what
the sea churns up—Here,
take it all back—cleaning
itself in winter storms,
shimmer shimmer everywhere.

2.

A knock came at my door
this place where I expected
no one but crow or gull
to cross my threshold
and I startled from daydream

to social self a twinge
of fear. There'd been
a rough guy maybe
meth inflected
dumped his pickup

on the seawall
a place no truck
was meant to be
and here I was
a woman alone

though older than
the customary prey
a woman knows
herself to be in
predatory minds.

We set alarms in our flesh
hard to shut off
even when nothing
poses danger.
You've got a visitor

the man said geared
up in sun-guard clothing
a face that had taken
too much wind and sun
but warm in greeting—

See if you needed
anything. Carolina
skiff lobbing
at the shore
a boat I knew

the man not yet
both tending salmon
in floating cages
wild smolts brought
here to be raised

and released
to the wild. Would
they return? Who knows
but native fish
need help and Irving—

people say the oil company
name as if saying
Jimmy or Bob—
needs to clean up
its reputation

if not the planet's
air so salmon
here are doing

double duty
for wild and corporate

needs. Only wild
salmon farm
in the world
he tells me.
Nicks their tails

to mark for DNA.
I can bring stuff in
or out for you.
Used to help the others.
Gives nod to half a dozen

shacks akimbo
on the wall. Brought
that propane stove
I think. Thanks.
Wind's the constant

visitor. Can't tell
what causes it
to whistle and
wail. Camp might
as well be adrift.

3.

I like the sounds of work.
Ring of hammer
hitting nail
as sound wave bounces
off the drumhead

of basaltic cliffs
and I batlike
echolocate
as if such music
were the meal I crave.

Splash of salmon
practicing its
upstream leap.
Gulping sound
when seal upends

to dive and water
swallows in its wake.
Crow call insisting,
its voice
meant be heard.

Hum of outboard,
dory dulse-loaded full
riding low and slow
back home. Muffled voices
of crew stringing twine

on Sea Dream weir.
I can even hear
the whisper of ink
rolling across the page,
work that feels like breathing.

4.

It was kind of a man camp
when I got it. Collection
of ball caps salvaged
off rocks and mounted
above the window frame.

Shur-Gain Aquaculture
Roland's Sea Vegetables
Led Zeppelin album covers
mounted on plywood wall
plus stippled poster

of The Jam—Jagger
Joplin Stevie Nicks
JohnPaulRingoGeorge
a hundred more
their faces made

mosaic by the artist's
hand. My friend
who built the place
tried to name them all.
Coffee mugs enough

for what company
might happen by
peering in to admire
the oil welled
in the lamp's glass base.

5.

One night we had a party.
This was after I'd
womaned up the place.
Flowered oilcloth to cover
the table's peeling veneer.

Dishtowel sporting
lobster trap and red
boiled victims thumbtacked
to the western wall.
Two new windows

to invite the light.
Friends came
by plastic rowboat,
ATV, and foot.
Wine and stories

flowed. I read
some poems
about storm petrels
and our dancer friend
played the part

illustrating with her limbs
the birds' forest burrowing
and their pelagic flight.
Funky as the camp still was—
doorknob rusted shut

by a winter's worth
of salty fog (we had to
climb in through
the sliding window)—
it felt like home.

When some neighbors
bellied up to the open
sill the dulse camp
felt like a swim-up bar
at some tropical resort.

Then everyone topped
over cobble to climb
the seawall and watch
sun's fall. Minke
passing by. Black sheen

diving into water's
plate glass. Sun dense
pink sliding from
cinematic gray clouds.
All meant to be seen.

6.

The sea will take it
of course
whether by one
engulfment or
slow erosion.

It was never meant
to last. Kind of a joke
about the pretense
of all we build.
Here. Not here.

And all we've done
to speed the going
under. But surely
it would have been a pity
not to have seen

spindly black spiders
that thrive in heaped
up stone no need
for frivolous greenery
just the intelligence of

knowing its place.
Oh, must we
keep making the world
uglier than it was
before we came

while asking
for more beauty?
Yes, a pity not to ponder
the otter and the osprey,
hear laughter

cross the water
from another camp
that comforting music
of Friday night and beer
kayak paddle dipping

stroke by stroke riling
glitter in its wake
and for a moment
to know whatever
you've suffered

whatever you've lost
here is a bed,
a quilt and pillow,
tea resting
on a driftwood stump.

THE COURAGE OF THE SAVANNAH SPARROW

Beside Great Pond where the gulls come
leaving the salt to bathe in fresh,
dunking and flapping and splashing
to lighten their wings, along a lane
lined with salt grass, sea oats,
and cow parsnip, the sparrow
chipped at me as I walked the dog.
The bird hopped ahead
seed tassel to seed tassel
anticipating my advance and with each hop
blasting an alarm call to warn me away.
I assume warn because Savannah sparrows
nest on the ground, thatching matted dried grass
into a cup lined with finer grass and tucked
under overhanging weeds so the bird
must tunnel in from one side.
This is the season when nestlings,
unable to fly, lie hidden and helpless
in that green shroud. But what
does a bird so small I could fit
three in my palm assume?
She should be terrified of me
for my size alone yet she continues
as I walk repeating and repeating
her one word as if teaching me
a language I am too slow to learn.

TANNIN, SKY, NIGHT

How to describe the color
of a pond gone fugue
in autumn wind
surface tinctured blue,
sky-stained and deeper water
tea-stained from steeping in peat
that netted entanglement
that took a thousand years
to form. How far the land
can go in telling
a story, water
dark as obsidian night
toward which I progress
every day feeling
endless longing to hold on.

IV

THE EXCAVATIONS

1. ACROPOLIS

What if there is no Ithaca
        only this drift
toward the dream
        arched windows
framed in limestone
        the sea's gift
to architecture
        an ancient wall
standing after history's
        keening
has gone silent:
        the beauty
of the ever open.
        Decapitated gods
line the stage
        of the Theater of Dionysus.
Scaffolding
        shields the Acropolis
for repair. Tourists throng
        a hiveless swarm
come to gather
        the honey of antiquity.
At night the modern city
        spills its light
upward so the sculpted rock
        seems to guard us
while we sleep. By day
        the Athenian cats
relax at home in the ruins
        sunwashing their fur
heads turning
        to follow sudden nothings.

2. *KARYATIDS*

I have trouble with the women
        not the cook who calls me mama
though I'm traveling with my grandson.
        She insists I make him eat,
he's too skinny look at the Greek men.
        He rolls his eyes.
I don't think she wants to hear
        about my esophageal stricture
that requires surgical stretching every five or ten years.
        No I get it she just wants to feed him
as I do by bringing him to Greece
        though he knows more about history
than I do explaining to me why 1453
        is the most important date
to remember. No, it's the women
        who hold the Temple of Athena
on top of their heads gowned
        as if carrying all that holy weight
were nothing to them so accustomed
        to their burdens and in their time
women not even citizens.
        They may be the women of Sparta
who hated death but loved war
        condemned to slavery
for being on the wrong side.
        They may be village dancers
who wear baskets of reeds on their heads
        their bodies mere
stalks that quiver
        with currents and wind.

3. *MYCENAE*

The tragedies are all
  just stories until
you've stood on the hilltop
  and surveyed the silver haze
of olive groves that descend
  all the way to the sea
the view from which Clytemnestra
  spent ten years sharpening
the blade of her vengeance.
  In faithless Agamemnon's
beehive tomb stone benches
  line the wall
for mourners to sit
  in their keening
the domed ceiling
  vaulted high to hold
their cries. Even now the dead
  stay three days
in their house while people
  come to sit and cry
professional mourners who can
  fill a vault with grieving.

Forest bees on these hillsides
  collect nectar
from the pines by way
  of aphids. The insects
feed on tree sap
  digest amino acids
and excrete sweets
  that bees gather

from aphid bodies—this amber
    honey in the jar
a story about how to find the sweets
    in the most bitter forest.

4. *EPIDAURUS*

We traveled with tourists
        from London   Dallas
the cat lady from Brisbane
        (skipped the ruins
to feed the ferals
        in every harbor)
and our Greek guides
        adept at history
(Persians attacked
        on horseback so Greeks
staged the battle
        in a marsh where
horses were useless)
        and afterhours
drinks on deck of our small ship
        where Ray laughed
with them until
        his face hurt.
They made good fun of everyone
        (the British—all teeth,
the Americans—all cowboy)
        and we felt our way
toward understanding
        their passion for democracy—
neo-Nazis elected
        in Greece after
all their people had suffered
        and died for—
that was their horror.
        How could it be

Yoseph begged to know
        that *here* such monsters
could be elected?
        We lay at anchorage
becalmed by the glow
        of cigarettes and liquor
halyards clapping against
        steel masts in the wind.

At Epidaurus we took turns
        clapping our hands
on stage to see if the echo
        would reach the back row
of the theater that nosebleed
        section high up
the hillside of limestone
        benches that
circle the stage like a giant
        megaphone
though the circle is broken
        to make room for
the proscenium. Aristophanes
        or Aeschylus
Sting as Sting or Helen Mirren
        as Phaedra.
But first the Asclepian sanctuary
        next door to heal the body's ills
snakes in the underground
        labyrinth bringing knowledge
to lighten the suffering.
        For those ills not described
by the body the way to cleanse
        spirit and mind

played out on stage
          stories so netted into psyche
they last six thousand years.
          Regimes tried to bury
the art—Goths and Romans
          then Ottoman Turks—
knowing art would keep
          the people alive.
Once rubble and neglect began
          to accrete
nature colluded piling scree
          and scrub that concealed
the genius of the place
          for centuries.

5. *DELPHI*

Our guide shared the story
        of a prophecy:
the queen told her two sons
        the brother who kisses
his mother first
        will be king.
One fell. The other stood
        and kissed her.
She chose the fallen one.
        Why
the other protested when
        I kissed you first?
Yes but your brother
        kissed Mother Earth.
It's a good story
        to tell at Delphi
where it took a woman
        to inhale the vapors
rising from a crack
        in the hide
of ragged Mt. Parnassus
        and speak truth
to priests though her words
        were unintelligible
so they made up
        what they wanted to hear
and called it prophecy.
        No matter. Walking
among those ruins
        rock nuthatches

singing loud all around
    it's impossible not to feel
the importance to the ones
    who prayed
and the ones who paid
    for the privilege
of asking questions
    there at the omphalos
where the surface opens
    to the depths. Goats
first identified the spot
    dancing drunk
in the fumes. You can feel
    the weight of time
layered like sedimentary rock
    Gaian worship to Pythian serpent
to Apollo that god of order
    harmony and music
who had to spend eight years
    as a mortal to be cleansed
after killing the python
    who guarded the site.
All buried under stone
    the old beliefs
so lost that peasants
    built the village of Kastri
out of the sanctuary's rubble.
    So hidden was Delphi
even its location unknown
    for centuries
that excavations only began
    in 1892. If not for

the persistence of stories
        the dig would never have begun
no pick or shovel or fox hair brush
        no slow reveal
no astonishment
        at what the excavations
exposed—art as healing grace.
        Ray and I arrived
at the Temple of Apollo
        from our separate
walks in the ruins
        sat on the stone wall.
It was nothing we'd planned
        or discussed. I saw him
rest his palms upturned
        on his knees and I
met his gesture with my own.
        We sat that way
at a distance in quiet
        palms raised
ready to receive
        the light that might
fall into them
        from that elevated air.

V

DEAR AMERICA

1.

Dear America, it's time you took a good look at yourself.
Saturday morning. Shopping at the Farmer's Market
in St. Phillip's Plaza. A vendor I visit every week
for tomatoes and romaine, beets and squash, whatever
she's offering that Arizona hard-till has offered her.
That's how things work in the plant-and-animal world
—give and take—even trees, we've learned, feed
one another through hidden filaments that partner with roots.

Such is the learning won through big time—what the ancients
divined through mythopoesis and we refine through science
and art. Everything is connected. So I'm reaching for my organic eggs
when these two young guys come up to the table and one starts asking,
What's this? Pointing to a patty pan squash. How do you cook it?
He sounds a bit tight and formal—something off in the tone. I turn
to see the Glock in its holster on his belt, his hand pushing t-shirt aside
to be sure the gun is visible. He doesn't want to buy anything.

He just wants to be seen. His gun buddy at his side. T-shirt forest green
untucked over khakis. Dark well-cut hair, fair skin, he might be a college student.
Is this a prank? Got the open carry permit just to see what he could
get away with? Research project, he and his buddy comparing notes?
Or is he the one, the clean-cut kid who has been plotting vengeance
against assaults he cannot name. Or does he really just want to be seen
for having a freedom no one is about to dispute? I see you, dude. Believe me.
Is that enough? Can I go now? But he lingers. And so do I to say I see.

2.

Dear America, if you make a wrong turn after leaving
the national park you end up at the wastewater site
where shit gets processed and cleaned and turned back
into good earth, you end up where rusted out trailers
bunch up in empty yards that look like it hasn't rained
in forever and a washboard dirt road leads you back
to the city, the southside where a highway named Garlic
welcomes you to the strip-mall-and-take-out American West.

If you can't find your way home from what feels like
desolation you can stop for directions at the Aztec café
where a warrior-priest rises from the brickwork,
quetzal headdress blazing like the sun's corona,
cars and pickups lined like horses at their hay,
a place of belonging in the land of the displaced,
everyone trying to piece together a meal and the hope
that you, Dear America, will take us all in your embrace.

3.

Dear America, it's time to let your civil war go. I'm sitting at the bar
local hipster breakfast place French toast with macerated berries and almonds,
sunny side eggs with olives, feta and roasted pepper sauce,
when a large party settles in at the table behind my back.
What makes me turn to see him, some sixth sense, as the muscled guy
wearing a Dropping Warheads on Foreheads t-shirt
unpacks a cardboard box then the hard-shell plastic case inside to show off
his new SIG or AK or Heckler—big black gun meant for most murder?

I fix eyes with another man at the table, a WTF? look and he tries
to make calm eyes at me but there they all are more than a dozen
the husbands and wives and a toddler climbing all over the parents
and everyone happy with holiday cheer because its Christmas Eve
and someone is getting a magnificent weapon this year which makes
at least one man very happy and proud. The others? I can't say.
They notice me noticing them. Probably veterans maybe Air Force.
They have had to do work they may never get over. *This shit*

is guaranteed to give you the freedom boner you deserve. Check out
the website for this and grosser taunts of the t-shirt's meme
the kind that worries me for the women at the table. Easy for me
to stare down the asshole who thinks breakfast in America
is a good time to whip out your SIG. Someone is going home
with this guy, someone is getting into bed with him, someone else
is unwrapping the present and getting hard imagining that its insignia
a shark's toothy grin inked onto a bomb speaks for his right to do harm.

4.

Dear America, please, it's time to feel the pain that underlies your cruelty
and tend to it. This was twenty years ago, the cabbie said. I was riding
with him to a hotel in Revere, Massachusetts. I was dancing at a club, he said,
with this beautiful Venezuelan girl. This was Boston. He'd been
in the city already six years. Puerto Rican, he said. He'd voted for Trump,
what his mother keeps telling him was the worst decision of his life,
so many suffering at home after the storm. Without water or power.
Venezuela helped. Brazil helped. Nothing from the U.S., he said.

I told him I live in Arizona—so much suffering on the border.
His mother, he said, says God doesn't want people to suffer like that.
That night in the club, he said, agents burst in, started rounding up people.
The Venezuelan was terrified. My 9-year-old daughter is home sleeping,
she whispered. I can't let them take me. He whispered back. Whatever they ask you
just say, Yes. Just say, Yes. He took her hand and walked up to the agents.
Are you a citizen? Yes, he said. I'm Puerto Rican and this is my wife. Yes, she said.
He held her hand. He saw her years later. She whispered, You saved my life.

5.

Dear America, let's take the ferry to the Statue of Liberty. Let's spread
our beach blankets out beneath the chains cut from her unshackled feet.
Let's bring the Coke and Sprint and Arizona Iced Tea.
Let's share potato salad and taquitos, hot dogs and tofurkey.
Let's sing the song we learned in high school and mean it:
Send these and I lift and golden shores. Bring your service dog and parakeet.
Your grandmother and the neighbor you dislike. Bring Kavanaugh McConnell
Hannity Ingraham. Tell them they can wear no make-up and no suit

and they can't say a word. But they must eat what's given and give thanks
with a nod. They must do the dishes and clean up the trash. They must count
how many dandelions have bloomed in the grass, how many gulls
have stopped by for a snack. Hey everyone, let's quiet them, the voices
that deceive and suppress and betray and lie. Let's show them
what language is for by making them hungry to connect. I know some
of you will want them to be your friends. That's not their job.
Their job is come to the picnic and help clean up the mess.

6.

Dear America, there's a strange artfulness to the performance
by the Patriot Front as they suit up in prep khaki, navy polos,
white gators cloaking smug grins. Cosplay militia
packed in a U-Haul. They never made it to Pride Day.
A neighbor made them. But conspiracy to riot is not art.
Better to fancy yourselves a Greek chorus and keen
for what you feel you've lost which now really will be
your freedom taken from you not by the drag queen

wearing a rainbow boa and entertaining the crowd in the park
but by your own lawless fantasy of what whiteness means
and what it wants. I'm white and I want no part of your
playdate with the collapse of civilization.
I took a long drive through the arid west
to clean my head, prickle poppies blooming white
in the median strip. Came to feed lots, stench of cattle
standing in their degradation awaiting death. Drove on

to Tulsa where I stayed beside the Creek Council Oak Tree,
a cottage with fenced yard for the dog, her joy and mine.
When the Muscogee Creeks arrived in 1836, reads the guest book,
after two years on the Trail of Tears they placed ashes
from their ancestral fires at the base of the tree and stayed.
Village business, ceremonies, celebrations all kept company
with the oak. They took the tree's council: rooting down,
holding ground, making shelter, thanks to the persistence of light.

7.

Dear America, I know it's hard to speak of how we've been
wounded. I mean all those children murdered in their school.
I mean the man stepped on by a cop for so long
he died under the fucker's foot while three other cops
stood watching. I mean four hundred years robbing people
of homeland, chaining them, breeding them, lynching them,
stripping them of culture, language, belonging, giving them
the massa's name. I mean the sunflower fields

in North Dakota where your nuclear arsenal lies buried
each silo surrounded with chain link and three strands of barb wire,
the missileers at work generation after generation memorizing
the launch codes then playing cards or writing poems (no lie—
I heard a poet ran a workshop in a Minot bar)—anything to stall
the boredom of another shift when nothing happens while they wait
for word to start the worst that can happen. Above them
tractors ply fields of blue flax and yellow mustard flower.

8.

Dear America, I know it's not enough to hate you for your failures.
Let's go back to the Farmer's Market on Sunday morning
and shop for late summer squash and fresh eggs spotted
with shit—you don't need to refrigerate these, the vendor says,
because they haven't been washed. Let's visit the booth
where the Kurds sell baklava, where the Navajos float
sage smoke over the professor's sciatica, where rusty steel
coyotes and quail can be bought for a song.

Let's try an Anjou pear and Moroccan pomegranate,
some Medjool dates and a lobster roll from Maine.
Let's have our Tarot cards read and buy some grass-fed beef.
Let's have nopales and tortillas while the sycamore leaves fall
like wedding confetti and the heat is finally abating in the desert
and no one is packing or baiting anyone into outrage
just for this one sacred hour when the heirloom tomatoes
are perfectly ripe and the dry river dreams itself full.

NOTES

"Galapagos"
I thank my grandson Lincoln for his good company on our trip to the Galapagos.

David Taylor's invitation to visit Cuba inspired "The Gardener's Creed." Our group of U.S. writers and ecocritics was hosted in Havana by the Antonio Nuñez Jimenez Foundation for Nature and Humanity, whose work fosters a Cuban society informed by environmental conscience. Since 1990 they have supported "people's plots," vacant state property set aside for people who want to grow food on urban ruins. For an historical view of Professor Felipe Poey y Aloy (1799-1891), I've relied upon "Sketch of Felipe Poey" by David Jordan, *Popular Science Monthly*, August 1884. I am indebted to Robert Duncan's poem "Often I am Permitted to Return to a Meadow." Formally, "The Gardener's Creed" roughly follows the Spanish *décima* form with ten-line stanzas and eight-syllable lines.

"Wild Apples"
Repurposes passages from Henry David Thoreau's eponymous essay.

"Two for the Moon"
At liftoff, Armstrong's heart rate was 110 beats per minute. On the moon landing, it was 156 beats per minute. When his boot touched the moon's surface, it spiked to over 200 beats per minute.

For "The Vocation of Care," thanks to Ellen Dore Watson who brought me to the Archibald MacLeish Field Station during my visit to Smith College.

"Field Studies: Kent Island." "First, There was an Albatross" is a title borrowed from Nathaniel Wheelright's 2014 article in *Bowdoin Magazine* telling the story of Ernest Joy's discovery of the albatross near Grand Manan Island and the establishment of the Bowdoin College

Scientific Research Station. J. Sterling Rockefeller wrote in *The Auk: Ornithological Advances* in 1933 about the expedition to the Congo to find Grauer's Green Broadbill. Rockefeller did in fact do something for the nesting eiders. He purchased Kent Island and donated it to Bowdoin College as a refuge for birds. In 1954 Chuck Huntington began his research on the Leach's storm petrels that nest in burrows on Kent. His work continued for fifty years. His obituary states that he "amassed longitudinal data on a single population of animals over an interval and at a level of detail that are perhaps without equal in field biology." At present the petrel study is the second oldest continuous data set in the world. About 25,000 petrel pairs currently nest on the island; of these about 75 pairs are tracked. The population has declined 30% since 2014. The work continues with ornithologists Bob Mauck and Mark Haussmann. An article by John M. Pearce on the philopatry (site faithfulness) of the petrel was published in *The Auk* in 2007. Nathaniel Wheelright has led Kent's research on savannah sparrow migration and breeding. Heather Williams currently studies the song culture of savannah sparrows. Patty Jones, current Director of the Field Station, conducts the work on the nectaring behavior of bees. Robert Cunningham, cloud physicist at MIT, came to the island in 1938 to study fog. He slept in a tiny cabin named Fog Heaven. The data he collected helped lead to the U.S. Clean Air Act of 1970. He painstakingly gathered data on Kent for 60 years. This sequence of poems, then, is something of a collaboration with a community of scientists who have devoted their working lives to learning what one remote little island in the Bay of Fundy has to teach us.

"The Wolves" repurposes a line from my essay "The Rabbit on Mars" in *Zoologies*: "the animals who were our first gods in the childhood of humanity."

"Looking for Lorca" is set in Granada, Spain. The poem's original title was "Self-Portrait Embracing a Fabulous Beast," taken from a drawing by Lorca that Miró said was a poem. But in the end, that was Lorca's title and not mine. Lorca's wandering theater group was La Barraca. YouTube offers a clip of them hitting the dusty roads to bring free performances to rural communities. https://www.youtube.com/watch?v=bM9-JFyPggQ

See also the documentary "Latticework of Trees." The "?Que es la vida" quote dates to about 1660 from "Monólogo de Segismundo" by Pedro Calderón de la Barca. All other italics are from Lorca.

Gratitude to Diana Villanueva Romero and the Spanish Association of American Studies for their invitation to speak in Cáceres and their hospitality in Extremadura.

"The Excavations" was informed by Ted Hughes's translation of *The Oresteia* by Aeschylus.

Thanks to my grandson Raymond for his good company on this adventure.

"The Dulse Camp" appropriates lines from Seamus Heaney's "Station Island" and Elizabeth Bishop's "Questions of Travel." With thanks to Elton Green for sharing his camp with me.

BIOGRAPHICAL NOTE

Alison Hawthorne Deming is the author of six books of poetry and five books of nonfiction, editor of the anthology *The Gift of Animals: Poems of Love, Loss, & Connection*. Among her awards are a Guggenheim Fellowship, NEA Fellowships, Stanford's Stegner Fellowship, and the Walt Whitman Award from the Academy of American Poets. Her writing has been widely published, including in the *Norton Book of Nature Writing* and *Best American Science and Nature Writing*. She is Regents Professor Emerita at the University of Arizona. She lives in Tucson, Arizona, and Grand Manan, NB, Canada.

www.ingramcontent.com/pod-product-compliance
Lightning Source LLC
LaVergne TN
LVHW091818191026
850458LV00033B/319